My Name is Medusa

a girl god publication

Written by Glenys Livingstone

Illustrated by Arna Baartz

Copyright 2016 Glenys Livingstone
All Rights Reserved

ISBN 978-1530922895

All illustrations are the property of Arna Baartz. All rights reserved. None of the illustrations may be reproduced or utilized in any form or by any means, electronic or mechanical, including photocopying, recording or by any information storage and retrieval system, without prior written permission from Arna Baartz.

www.thegirlgod.com

Other Girl God Books for Children

The Girl God
A book for children young and old, celebrating the Divine Female by Trista Hendren. Magically illustrated by Elisabeth Slettnes with quotes from various faith traditions and feminist thinkers.

Mother Earth
A loving tribute to Mother Earth and a call to action for children, their parents and grandparents. Written by Trista Hendren / Illustrated by Elisabeth Slettnes.

Tell Me Why
A feminist twist of the creation story told with love from a mother to her son, in hopes of crafting a different world for them both.

My Name is Inanna
Tamara Albanna weaves the tale of Inanna's despair, strength and triumph—giving children of all ages hope that the dark times in life will pass. Arna Baartz illustrates this journey with gorgeous paintings of the owls, lions, stars, sun and moon that direct Her. *My Name is Inanna* is dedicated to Tamara's beloved homeland, Iraq—The Cradle of Civilization; the Land of the Goddess.

My Name is Lilith
Whether you are familiar with the legend of Lilith or hearing it for the first time, you will be carried away by this lavishly illustrated tale of the world's first woman. This creative retelling of Lilith's role in humanity's origins will empower girls and boys to seek relationships based on equality rather than hierarchy.

My Name is Isis
A fresh look at the ancient Egyptian Goddess, Susan Morgaine reclaims Isis as The Great Mother Goddess and The Giver of Life, from whom all things come. Arna Baartz mystically illustrates Her as healer and protectress. *My Name is Isis* is a treasure box for children of all ages who want to draw close to this wise and nurturing Mother Goddess.

My Name is The Morrigan
The Morrigan remains one of the most misunderstood goddesses of the Celtic pantheon. Her mythology is a tangled web of various guises, deeds, and battles--and even her name is a bit of a mystery! Dive into the world of the Goddess of Death, and learn about what The Morrigan really has to teach us--and, maybe you'll find that She, and death, aren't so scary after all!

My Name is Venus of Willendorf
Today more than ever, the image of the Venus of Willendorf is a relevant one. Women and girls are bombarded with Photoshopped images of an "ideal" body shape that is quite literally unattainable. Remembering Willendorf's powerful story reminds us of the beautiful abundance of the female body, with all of her hills and valleys, lush softness, and fertility. You don't want to miss this body-positive celebration of the Great Mother Goddess!

More Praise for My Name is Medusa

"A wonderful introduction to and re-framing of the myth of the wise, powerful, fabulously snaky-haired Medusa. The magical pages of this gorgeous book teach children love for the Earth and for all of Her creatures." -Miriam Robbins Dexter, Author of *Whence the Goddesses: a Source Book*

"I am awe struck at the beautiful job you have done in liberating Medusa from the stereotype, and elevating Her to a rightful place among the deities. You have spoken in poetic and innocent language, a re-enchantment of "the dark" that will lead us all, child and adult, into the soft warm darkness of the womb, the earth, and the cosmos. I will make it my business to be sure that little black girls in my circle of concern get to read and discuss the content of this work and to feast their eyes upon the exquisite artwork. Thank you for this masterpiece."-Yeye Luisah Teish, Yoruba Priestess, Teacher and Author of *Jambalaya: The Natural Woman's Book of Personal Charms and Practical Rituals*

Praise for My Name is Inanna

"Full of meaning and insight, with stunning illustrations, this simple, poetic version of the ancient myth glimmers like the "inner star" the author describes, showing where to turn for guidance." -Marilyn McFarlane, Author of *Sacred Myths: Stories of World Religions*

"The Girl God does it again with this inspiring, lyrical read! In *My Name is Inanna*, Tamara Albanna and Arna Baartz team up to bring the goddess of love to life for even the youngest readers. As human children, we will all face times of struggle and darkness in our lives. The powerful story of Innana, as told in these pages, reminds us that we too can trust ourselves and let our own inner star of intuition guide our way. An important message for us all!" -Melia Keeton-Digby, Author of *The Heroines Club: A Mother-Daughter Empowerment Circle*

Praise for My Name is Lilith

"At a time when the rising light of the sacred feminine appears to be suddenly slipping backwards into the shadows, this book is vitally relevant. Lilith, the forgotten first companion of Adam, tells her own love story, and in doing so empowers us to step into the fullness of our divine selves."-Mirabai Starr, Author of *Caravan of No Despair*

"I love everything about this book. It is simply enchanting and carries an important message, one I want my own granddaughters to hear." -Jean Raffa, Author of *The Bridge to Wholeness*

DEDICATION:
To the Creative Dark

My name is Medusa.

People have said that I must be bad,
because I have snakes for hair.

But I don't think snakes are mean.

They are very clever, which is why I like them on my head.

I will tell you what fascinates me about them.

Snakes shed their skin all at once –
and get a new one again.

Humans shed their skin too, but
not all at once. It comes off
slowly, so you might not notice;
but when you are in the bath,
scratch your skin a little
and see.

All the cells of your body
are always changing,
like snake's skin.

Every seven years, you are a whole new outfit ~ inside and out ~ every bit of your body changed!

Humans never stay the same.

So it seems that you can always
change things you want to.

Snakes help remind me of that.

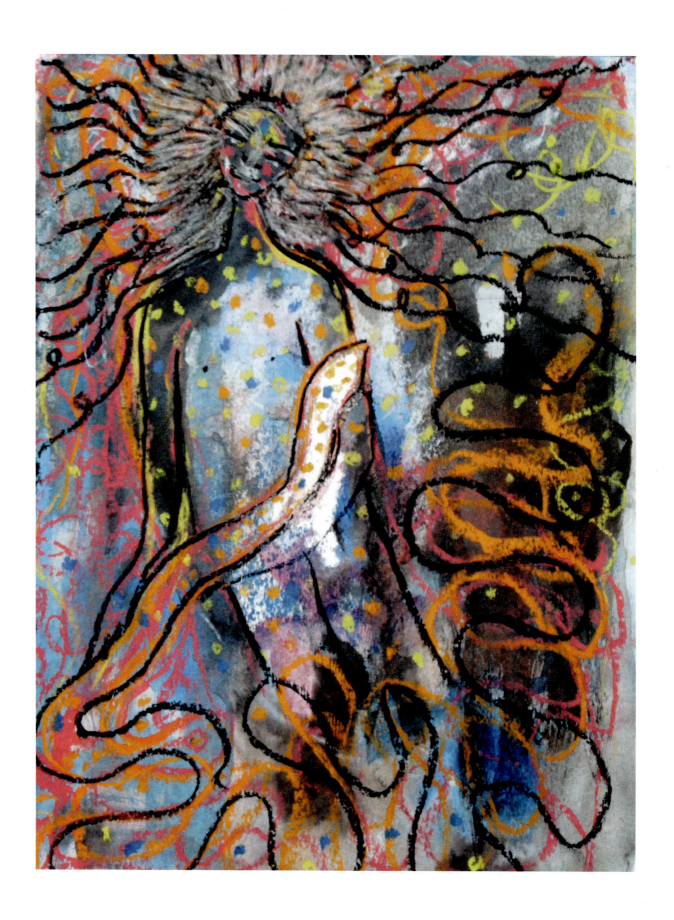

Snakes live under the surface of Earth.
Have you ever been there – in a cave?

Earth is alive and magical – She makes things grow.

So creatures that live inside Earth
must know special things.
They see the inside and the outside.

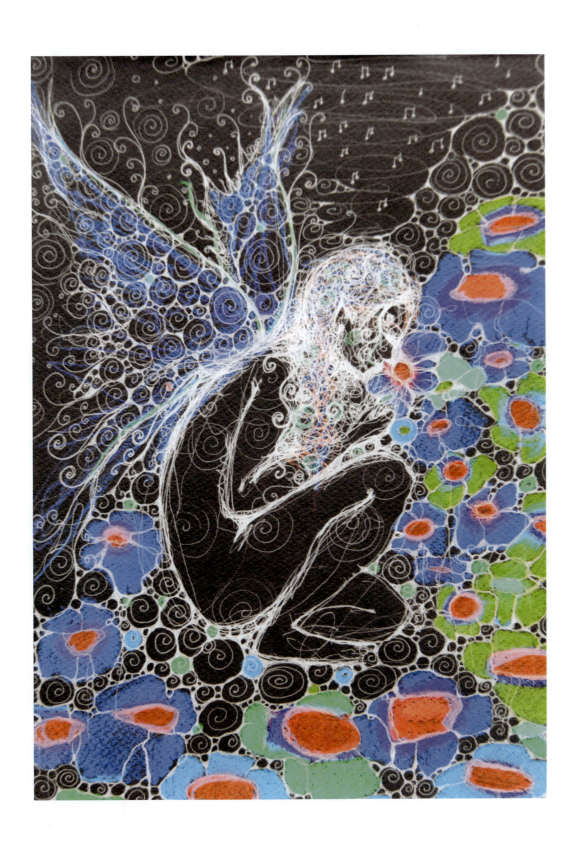

That's more than you and I see usually,
so I want to learn from them.

I also like snakes because
they can look out at the world constantly
without blinking.
You try doing that!

Being able to watch everything
for that long, quietly,
not saying anything,
can help you become wise.

I remember that
when I see my snakes.

Some people are afraid of wise things.
I'm not.

Children are wise in a kind of way you know.

Older people can be wise
in a different kind of way.
We can all be wise in our own
kind of way.

Another reason
that some people
are afraid of me is because I'm
not scared of the dark.

I love the darkness of the night
because you can see the moon and the stars.

I love to watch the moon change each night.

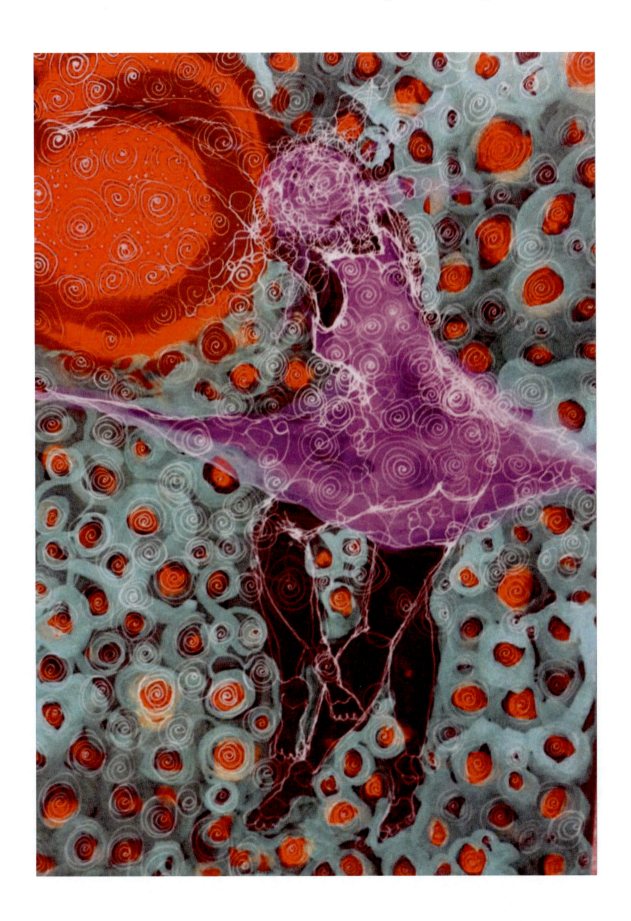

I love to look at the stars, and let their light into me.

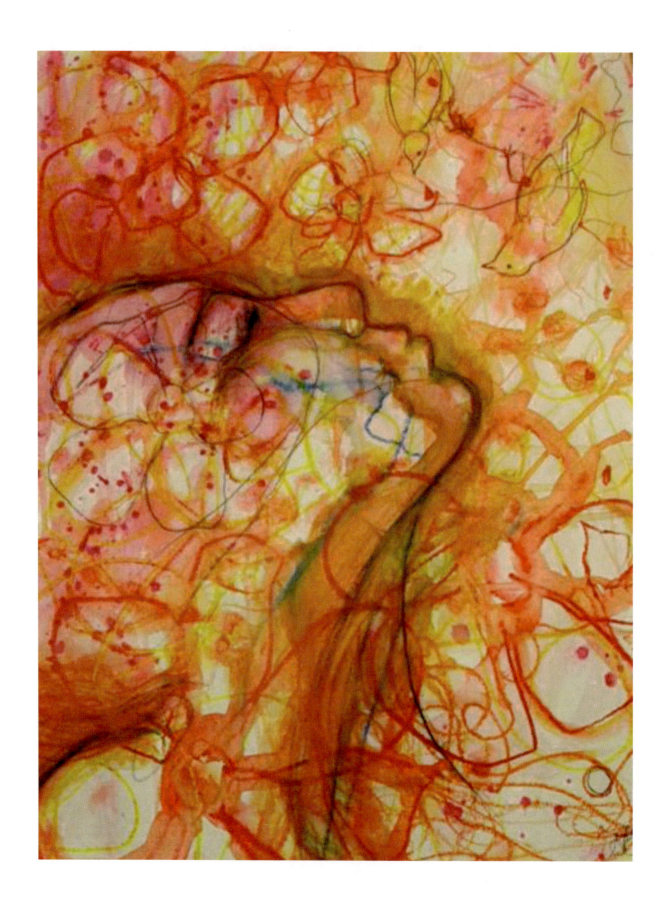

I feel they are part of me somehow.

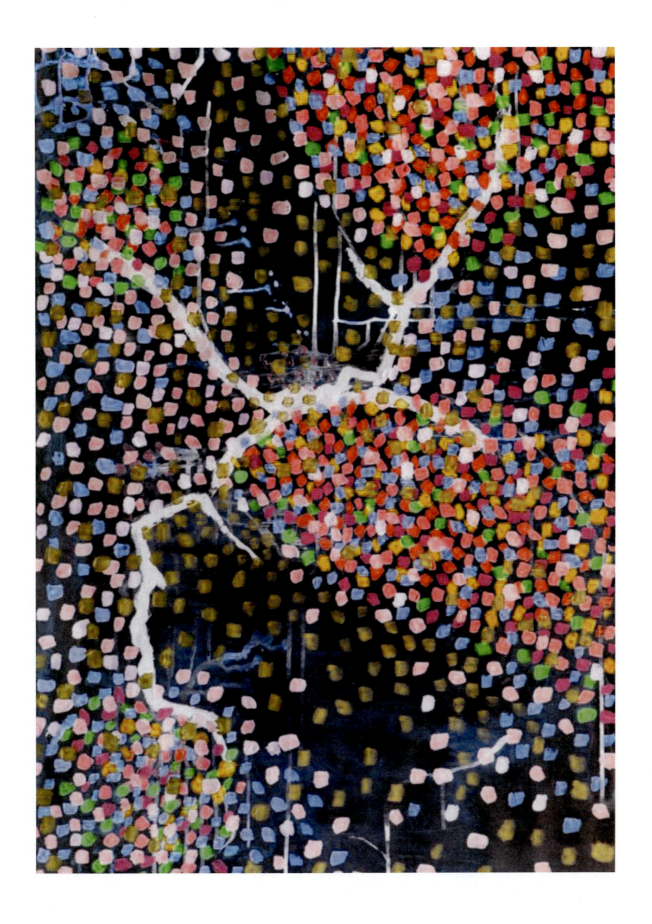

Try watching them yourself, and
imagine their light coming right into you.
See how you feel.

I also like to try to think of how
many stars there are.
Have you tried counting them?

Then I like to think about how far away the stars are.
For instance, the nearest star to our Sun is
41 million million kilometres away.
Try to imagine that!

When you do, your mind becomes
filled with the vastness of the Universe,
which is a good thing.

I also like the dark because it helps things grow.
When you put a seed in
the ground, the seed likes the dark
Earth, and it grows.

It grows into whatever it is
supposed to, but its roots always
stay in the dark earth,
giving it food.

You grow a lot in the dark too –
at night, in your sleep – like a seed
that's been planted.
Your body has time then.

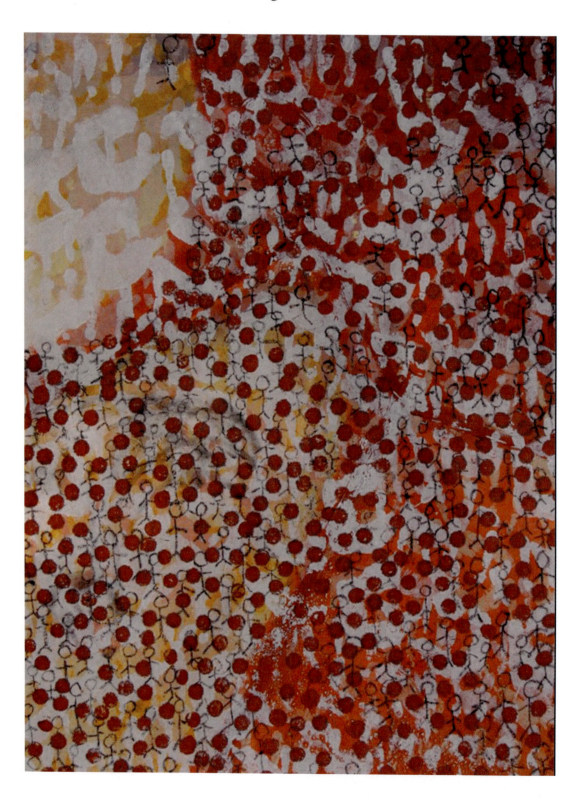

Even when you get big like me
you grow a lot at night – in a different way – in your dreams.

Your dreams keep telling you things you need to know,
and they happen best in the night.

Do you remember your dreams?

I like the way things quieten down at night;
everyone is not so busy.

Do you know what else the dark reminds me of?

When I was a tiny little thing inside my mother, it was so warm and safe in there. So now if I'm having a hard time, I try to make it feel like that again. I wrap myself up and lie still in the dark, like I was a tiny little thing; which I am in the eyes of the great big Universe ...
and in some mysterious way I begin to feel better again.

The dark has its own way of caring,
and coming up with something new.

Next time you hear my name,
remember all the good things I told you about myself.

And maybe
you can think of some more.

Glenys' Acknowledgements:

I thank the mothers and the grandmothers of the ages, who have spoken to me in some deep way beyond my knowing. Specifically regarding Medusa, there was the ovarian writing of Hélène Cixous, Patricia Reis and Patricia Monaghan. Yet there were many more women who re-membered the Dark Goddess for me – by Her many names – who helped me welcome Her back into the Creative communion with Her sister qualities of Young One and Mother. Much of that re-storying of Her is told in my book *PaGaian Cosmology* (2005), and was facilitated in Re-Storying Goddess classes, which I initiated and still sometimes teach. These circles were birthed in the early 1990's, thanks largely to the inspiration of woman activist and poet Marie Tulip; they have been sacred spaces in which all present in-formed each other with new Goddess research, images, story, meditations and ceremony.

I am thankful for the sciences that I learned, at first in secondary school, and always loved – astronomy, geology, physiology, biology, chemistry and physics; and I also loved poetry. I am thankful to physicist Brian Swimme for bringing poetry and science together, so that I could reach for expression of Her as Creative Dynamic unfolding the Cosmos.

I am thankful to all those who have been my teachers – for the compost and the gold; without whom I could not have known how essential the dark is for seeing the stars, the constellations by which to guide my path ... how the essential Dark may clear the past and nurture new being.

I am thankful to the future, the descendants of body, mind and spirit who called to me and urged me on.

I am thankful to the sentient Cosmos, dark and mysterious, whom I call Mother.

Arna's Acknowledgements:

For my powerful friend Monique with her beautiful, snaky hair and balanced heart. Since knowing you, dark and light have been rendered indistinguishable.

Stay tuned for the upcoming Anthology, *Re-visioning Medusa: from Monster to Divine Wisdom*, edited by Glenys Livingstone, Ph.D., Trista Hendren, and Pat Daly - and for more Children's books about Goddesses!

www.thegirlgod.com

Color Me!

It takes courage to dare to look at Her, to receive Her and conceive Her gift.

Made in the USA
Middletown, DE
26 February 2022